In
Search
of Deeper
Things
in Life

Sharmila
Panirselvam

WESTBOW
PRESS®
A DIVISION OF THOMAS NELSON
& ZONDERVAN

WestBow Press books may be ordered through booksellers or by contacting:

WestBow Press
A Division of Thomas Nelson & Zondervan
1663 Liberty Drive
Bloomington, IN 47403
www.westbowpress.com
844-714-3454

ISBN: 978-1-6642-4370-5 (sc)
ISBN: 978-1-6642-4371-2 (e)

Library of Congress Control Number: 2021917683

Print information available on the last page.

WestBow Press rev. date: 11/18/2021

Contents

Contents

1

MY BEGINNINGS

I WAS BORN AND RAISED IN A BEAUTIFUL FAMILY IN Malaysia. Ever since I was in my early teens, I was keen on God and His existence. I had a problem with death and dying. The question was, *What will happen if my parents die or if I die?* The next question was, *Why was I born into this world?* Then the questions went on with, *Why are some people born without arms and legs, blind and deaf, and many other congenital disabilities?*

I usually feel sorry and sad for people with such afflictions. Sometimes I think about it when I go to bed at night. There are days I am anxious and terrified about taking my last breath, dying, and leaving everyone behind, especially my loved ones and my parents.

My dad taught me how to pray, and he also reads the Mahabharata scriptures to me. Mahabharata is a Hindu scripture, and we are a Hindu family. The scriptures teach about implementing its spiritual precepts in everyday life. Long story short, all I wanted was for God to talk to me, give me the answers to my burning questions, and draw me close to Him. I used to attend Friday prayer in the temple. My mom encouraged me to pray to other Hindu goddesses as well, to guide me in my studies and my health, and to lead me to the right man to ensure my marriage was not delayed beyond a certain age. There are many goddesses, and each god serves a different purpose in life.

I used to kneel and pray in front of the Hindu altar in my house. I asked God to talk to me and show me the direction I should go in my life. Every day without fail, I said a prayer, or what some may call it a mantra, but something was missing. I could not hear God.

One day, a Chinese friend spoke to me about Taoism. This Chinese friend said that Taoism was a true religion, and I would see God's manifestation in a light form. I was a teenager seeking and pursuing God, and I thought maybe Taoism was a true religion and God would show Himself to me. I told my dad about Taoism and became a vegetarian. My dad was unhappy with that decision. Because I was still living under his roof, he said I should follow the set rules and regulations for being a Hindu and eating everything my mom cooked. At that time, I was seventeen years of age.

I had no choice but to let it go and follow my parents' will. The pursuit of God continued because I was insecure about where my life was heading. Quietly in my bedroom, I pondered this matter. Living in a Muslim country, Malaysia, also influenced me into Islam. The school I attended was almost 90 percent Muslim, and the Islam religion was taught in the classroom. Instead of going to the library during that subject being taught in the classroom, which was an option, I stayed in the classroom and did my homework.

The teacher who taught the subject touched on all the other religions and concluded that Islam was the true religion. I started to believe that I had found the one true God, and that was Allah. Secretly I told myself that I would convert to Islam and be free with my God when I was much older, independent, and no longer living with my parents.

Life went on after that. I kept my secret to myself because my dad expected me to obey him as to my religion. Shortly after completing high school, I applied to enter the nursing program. Everything went smoothly, and I was selected after the interview. While in nursing school, I continued attending Friday prayers in the Hindu temple. Even though I thought about Islam, I was not ready yet, but I would do it when I was much older. Meanwhile in that Friday prayers I asked God to show me the way and give me wisdom in life.

While in nursing school, I saw more human suffering in the hospital when doing my clinical with real patients. I applied my theoretical knowledge in clinical practice with guidance from a tutor. I questioned myself about God, His existence, and human suffering and sickness on earth.

As soon as I completed the three years of training, I immediately worked in a medical center not too far from my parents' home. Of the first salary I earned, I gave my mom half of the money. I did this due to my love for my parents and in remembrance of everything they did for me when I was a child. Besides that, I was from a middle-class family, and I had seen my dad sacrifice for us, even having little money. I used the rest of the money to pay for my rental apartment and enjoy my time with friends. I started going to nightclubs and dancing with my friends the whole night. I started drinking hard liquor, and it made me feel happy and free.

Though I had the money to do whatever made me happy, I was unfulfilled deep down in my heart. Something was missing in my life. Again I pondered upon the existence of God. I started questioning where I would go from here after my life on earth ended. I thought that now I might understand the Hindu religion by reading the Mahabharata scripture by myself. One weekend, I went to my parents' home and took the Mahabharata book with me to my apartment. I started reading page by page, but I was stuck with little understanding and was frustrated. I put the book aside, went on with my working life, and continued bar hopping on the weekends with my friends. I got to meet new people, and life went on for a while in that circle.

After five years of working in Malaysia, I left for Saudi Arabia for more money and more clinical experience as a staff nurse. Many of my coworkers were in Saudi Arabia, which influenced me to follow in their footsteps. When I was there, suddenly the secret I had kept to myself about converting to Islam vanished from my heart. I was not attracted to Islam anymore. I was more into making money and building my career. I had my own mission: to work in Saudi Arabia for a few years, and then I would make my journey to the United Kingdom and live in London. I was in Saudi Arabia for a total of six years. Upon coming to the end of my six-year journey, I applied for a job in the United Kingdom. I fill out the UK-required nursing board papers.

After completing the application, I put the papers aside in a secured drawer.

I took a short vacation home to Malaysia. While on that short vacation, I saw an advertisement in a newspaper that said, "Come and experience nursing in America." It offered a short meet-and-greet interview with a long-term travel nursing agency in California, whose representative came to recruit nurses in Malaysia. The agency offered an eighteen-month travel nursing contract in places across the world.

I attended the brief interview from the travel agency and filled out a form expressing my interest in applying for the program. It was a scholarship program, so I had nothing to lose if my application was not accepted. On the same day, there was an exam similar to the National Council Licensure Examination (NCLEX), which mimics the nationwide examination for nurses' licensing in the United States. Because I was already a practicing nurse in Malaysia, I had no problem passing the exam the first time I took it. After passing that test, I was given application papers to start the process of coming to America.

There was a requirement that those from non-English-speaking countries must take an English test. I doubted that I will pass the first time but surprisingly I scored a 'pass' on the International English Language Testing System (IELTS), and three months later, I took the actual NCLEX and passed the test without any issues. Then the screening process started. I had an interview with one of the hospitals in Southern California via phone and got the job in a critical care unit right away. Everything seemed to be going smoothly, and I decided to withdraw my application to go to the UK. The sponsorship from the travel agency in America seemed to be a good deal. In my heart, I said, *I will stay in America for two years, the length of the travel contract. Then I will make my journey to the United Kingdom.* It was a travel opportunity for me to see several countries by having a job in each country I would travel to.

In November 2008, I arrived in California. Many adjustments had to be made, and it was a stressful period—new country, new people, new system, learning to drive a car, and more. I did not see or meet any Malaysian people like I had when I was in Saudi Arabia. Nor did I meet people from my home city.

While adjusting to my new situation, I met my new coworkers, and we became friends. A nurse from Trinidad and Tobago used to invite me to her house; we usually had lunch or dinner together. I encountered nurses from other countries and became friends with them as well.

In the midst of adjustment in a new country, I said to myself, *This is also the time for me to start my spiritual life.* I still felt empty inside, and my fear about death and dying and where I would go from here returned. I was looking for a temple to go to where I could start learning more about my Hindu religion. I thought about getting one-to-one coaching from a teacher. When I was in Malaysia, I heard a spiritual leader by the name of Amma. Her actual name is Mata Amritanandamayi, but she is better known as Amma, which means Mother in English. She is revered as a hugging saint by her followers, because she gives comfort through hugs. I wanted to attend her classes in America, and I was looking for information so I could sign up for an online class. I bought some Hindu items to build an altar in my apartment.

I grew serious about looking for answers to all the burning questions about life. I was thirty-four years old at the time. Even though I was brand-new in America, I felt like time was passing fast, and I needed to start my spiritual journey. During that journey of searching, I continued working and going out with my new friends. Some friends invited me to go to church on Sunday, but I refused and told them I was a Hindu and I pray at home.

A friend from Trinidad and Tobago invited me to go out with her and her husband. We were to have dinner in a restaurant that Sunday evening. Before we reached the restaurant, her husband stopped at a building, and my friend said, "Let us go in here first, and then we will go for dinner."

When I entered the building, people welcomed us. In my head, I knew this was a church. I was extremely disappointed with my friend and thought, *How could she do this to me? She is rude for not respecting that I am a Hindu.* I was furious, but I kept silent, and my friend said, "It will be quick, and then we will have dinner."

I was even angrier and felt intimidated that we were in the front seats in the church. Soon the worship through music began. I was not impressed and could not wait for everything to be over.

I sat down after the worship. The pastor announced some events that would happen the next week. After that, he called his assistant pastor to preach for the evening. In my anger and disappointment with my friend, suddenly I was pulled into the message about the purpose of life and human existence, death and dying, who God is, and why Jesus came to earth as a man. It also touched every aspect of my life. I felt some warmness going through my body and could not take my eyes and ears from what the pastor was preaching. I melted down and wanted to kneel right away at my seat.

Many thoughts went through my mind, including the questions I had had when I was a teenager. I was desperate to know about the existence of God. In that twenty-minute sermon, all the burning questions I had were answered. At the end of the sermon, the pastor wanted the people to bow their heads and close their eyes for prayer. I did as instructed and gave my heart to Jesus that night.

My friend, sitting next to me, touched my shoulder and asked whether I was sleeping with my eyes closed. I said no, but I had done what the pastor asked us to do by bowing our heads and closing our eyes for prayer.

My friend said, "Okay, church is over. Let us have dinner now."

I quickly asked my friend whether I could follow her next Sunday to this church. She was so glad, and she said she would come get me, and we would go together.

The next Sunday, when I attended church with my friend, I received Jesus into my heart by confessing it through my mouth word by word, repeating after the pastor. I cried while saying the words that I received Jesus as my Lord and Savior. One more time, I felt warmness went through my body, and I felt at ease and peaceful. I wanted more and more information about the Lord Jesus, and I wanted the feeling of warmness to remain for as long as possible.

2

MY NEW LIFE

I LOVE THE CHURCH I ATTENDED, WHICH WAS A PENTECOSTAL church. I started to read the Bible that my friend gave me as a gift. The Word of God in the Bible makes me feel attached to Him, and I wanted to read more and more daily. The first few days after receiving Christ in my heart, I dreamed about my past in Malaysia and Saudi Arabia. I saw myself in the dream, like watching a video of my own life. I saw the same kind of dream repeated at least twice. I did not ask anyone in the church for the dream's meaning, but I felt like the old man was being removed and the new man was being put on.

I dreamed a lot at the beginning of my life with Christ. The same dream was being repeated as I walked in the new life. Even though I did not understand much about being born again at that time, it seemed like I was born again to this world and started new or fresh. The doubt and fear that I had had all my life vanished during that twenty-minute sermon on that one Sunday evening. I asked myself, *wow, Isn't this a miracle?*

I hungered to know more about Jesus. I read the Bible, attended church every Sunday, and went to Bible study on Thursday. I even started fasting three days a week. For people who have gone through desperation about something in life, when they get the solution, it is like winning the lotto, and they hold on to that one thing dearly. Every day and every minute, they cling to that precious possession. That is how I would describe what happened to my life.

I started to view things differently, and I wanted to do it all in Jesus's way. Shortly after receiving Christ in my heart in December 2008, I was baptized in water in June 2009. I felt so good because I was looking forward to the baptism by water. The pastor mentioned speaking in tongues as one of the evidences of being filled with the Spirit. I was also very eager to study the topic of being filled with God's power and speaking in other tongues. Even though I already had the Holy Spirit as a new believer, receiving the gift and speaking in tongues made me feel like I would soar with my Lord to another level.

I seek Jesus fervently every day. In my heart, it feels like I have found the love of my life. At thirty-five years of age, I was still single, but the Lord seemed to be enough for me. I felt like He was closer than anyone else around me. I started cleaning my apartment to ensure only the things approved by the Lord Jesus would be kept in it. I threw away the Hindu altar stuff I had bought when I had arrived in America. I also threw away any self-help books that I had and any suspicious-looking pictures or decor in my apartment. After doing that, I felt so good, and I started to fill the apartment with Bible scriptures. In every corner of my apartment, I have scriptures to help me remember the Word of God.

3

WALKING WITH THE LORD

VERY PERSON HAS A DIFFERENT ENCOUNTER WITH JESUS. Some people find Jesus in the most vulnerable situation they face. Some had a near-death experience. Some even died and met Jesus face-to-face. Others found Him when going through end-stage sickness in their bodies or other life situations. I believe this is all ordained by the Lord Jesus as to how people come to know Jesus and give their lives to this one true God.

In my story, it was simply by going out with a friend and not knowing that I would end up in a church. Jesus already knew that I was seeking God and was desperate to know about God's existence. Therefore, He used my coworker friend to help me to meet Him in a church. I have not seen Jesus face-to-face, but the preaching of the Word of God by the pastor and the feeling of warmness that washed over me and made me know that Jesus is God, and He was with me right there in the church. My mind was clear, and my heart was filled with love. I said to myself, *Wow, what an encounter with the one true God.*

In February 2010, I joined the twenty-one days of corporate fasting and prayer with my church. I sought God more and asked Him to give me the gift of speaking in tongues for my personal prayer life. I spent time in worship and then in praying aloud, but nothing happened. I yielded to God and allowed Him to give me whatever He wanted me to have as spiritual gifts.

At work one day, I started singing in an unknown language. It was during the twenty-one days of fasting and prayer. I knew this must be it. My words in the unknown tongue were few, but I was so excited and continued to sing throughout my work shift. I have been singing in the unknown tongue ever since then. I gained more words after that, and after the twenty-one days, I was able to pray in my secret language. I was amazed at what God would do for me if I sought His gifts without giving up.

When I pray, I worship God in the English language mixed with the secret language, and it is fulfilling. My relationship with Jesus grew even stronger, and I said, "Do whatever you want, Holy Spirit, because I want to fulfill the perfect will of my heavenly Father." I continued to pray, fast, and seek God like never before.

I told my Hindu parents that I was now following Jesus, and He is my God and Savior. Surprisingly, there was no resistance or anger toward me. My dad said that I would have a beautiful life because I have chosen to be with a good man, Jesus, and I should not be influenced by another way of living, such as an addiction to drugs, alcohol, the bad company of people, having sex with multiple partners, and more. My dad believes that Jesus is a godly man but is not God and Savior.

My dad felt I would do well in America because I have chosen to follow Jesus's ways. I told my dad that Jesus is the one true God, and everyone at home should be following Him. My dad said he is happy with being Hindu, and he believes God is with him as well. I have tried to convince my family that Jesus is the one, but I have failed, at least up until now. Since then, my mission is to pray for my entire family in Malaysia every day without fail that they will encounter Jesus one day. I have left this matter in the power of God to accomplish.

4

JESUS IS EVERYTHING

Ever since I met Jesus, I see life from a different perspective. Every morning, I wake up with a thankful heart that God spared my life and that I have another day to praise, worship, and walk with my Lord Jesus. My prayer life has grown stronger. Whatever I do, whether eating or drinking, I do it for the glory of God (1 Corinthians 10:31). With the words I speak, how I treat people, working under authority at work, honoring my parents, and in every little thing that I do, I want to honor God and walk in His ways.

I am not exaggerating, but every minute I am alive counts because the Lord is the ultimate life giver. I praise Him frequently and sometimes constantly because I know my Savior is walking so closely with me.

On my days off work, I get together with other Christian

friends for fellowship in my apartment. During that fellowship, I can really sense the presence of God. When every mouth praises and worships Jesus, after a few minutes, I feel someone tapping my shoulder. I feel like my hands and legs are pulsating and I have a heartbeat throughout my body. One time, I felt like a little earthquake occurred on the spot where I sit while worshipping God with other Christians. When that little earthquake happened, I got scared and opened my eyes because I thought there was really an earthquake. I saw the other friends still in worship mode, and their eyes were all closed. I wondered whether they realized there had just been an earthquake. I live in California, so I have experienced a few small earthquakes, which are frightening. I continued to worship God with my eyes closed.

After prayer, I shared the experience of an earthquake I had felt while worshipping the Lord Jesus. One of my friends explained that it must have been the power of God that came down and made me feel like an earthquake was happening. Each time I got together with fellow Christian friends, I also felt warmness surrounding me, and I was filled with joy and peace. I knew it was Jesus who was there, because in Matthew 18:20 it says, "For where two or three are gathered together in my name, there am I in the midst of them." I realized that our God is a living God, and God's Word is not a lie. I continued to get to know my one true God in even more personal and intimate ways.

5

MY LORD TALKS

As I walked intimately with the Lord, one day during my fasting and prayer time, I asked the Lord what He wants to do in my life. I told the Lord I wanted to know the plan and purpose He has for me. I repeatedly prayed the same thing every day but failed to know the specific plans and purpose the Lord has for me.

One day during my morning worship and prayer in my apartment, I heard it from my heart. Clearly the Lord said, "Feed My underprivileged children." I opened my eyes from the prayer and knew right away that I must feed His starving children in many parts of the world.

I did not hear any audible voice, but I heard it in my silent prayer, and the voice was a silent voice from my heart. I started searching for a Christian organization where I could contribute my offering in the form of money to feed these kids. I asked my church pastor whether the congregation contributes money and food to starving kids anywhere in this nation or other nations. He said the church's money goes to the work carried on by the church. The church helps the widows and contributes to education for underprivileged kids. I was happy with what my home church was doing, but I wanted to obey the specific instruction given to me by my Lord.

I continued looking for a Christian organization that helps feed kids who need food. I prayed for the Lord to show me the right organization. It went on for weeks with my prayer to ensure I would be giving to the right ministry.

God showed me the answer after weeks of praying for it. One morning after prayer, I went on YouTube to look for worship songs and sermons to help me listen to the Word of God, and I came across one of the Christian ministries in Texas that carries out its mission to feed children on several continents. I knew in my heart that I should help by contributing money to this ministry for the feeding mission. Ever since that day, I have contributed to that ministry. I realized if God gives you a task to do so, He will also show you the way or provide the resources you need to accomplish the task. The Lord will help if you obey His instruction. The Holy Spirit is the ultimate guide and teacher, and He speaks in a still, small voice.

6

HUNGRY FOR MORE OF HIM

A T ONE POINT IN MY LIFE, I WAS DESPERATE TO KNOW
about the existence of God, and after Jesus came
into my heart and revealed that He is the one true God,
my hunger to know Him more never stopped. I learned
to understand the Trinity, which consists of the heavenly
Father, the Lord Jesus, and the Holy Spirit. The heavenly
Father sent Jesus into this world to model the way of living
a holy life and to die on the cross so that humans could
have their sins forgiven and receive eternal life. Jesus is 100
percent God and became a human as well while He was on
earth. Baby Jesus was born to Mary, a virgin chosen by the
heavenly Father. Before the event of pregnancy took place,
an angel appeared to Mary one day; the angel Gabriel was
sent by the heavenly Father to earth to deliver a message
to Mary, and the angel said, "Rejoice highly favored one,

the Lord is with you; blessed are you among women!" (Luke 1:28). Mary was troubled and afraid. The angel said to her, "Do not be afraid, Mary, for you have found favor with God, and behold, you will conceive in your womb and bring forth a son and shall call His name Jesus. He will be great and will be called the Son of the Highest, and the Lord God will give the throne of His Father David. And He will reign over the house of Jacob forever, and of His kingdom, there will be no end" (Luke 1:30–33).

"Mary was shocked by the message and asked the angel, 'How can this be since I do not know a man?' The angel answered and said to her, 'The Holy Spirit will come upon you, and the power of the Highest will overshadow you; therefore, also, the Holy One who is to be born will be called the Son of God'" (Luke 1:34–35). "Mary replied to the angel by saying, 'Behold the maidservant of the Lord! According to your word, let it be to me,' and the angel departed from her" (Luke 1:38).

While Jesus was on earth, He foretold His crucifixion and resurrection to His disciples (Matthew 17:19). Then in John 16:7–15, Jesus went on to say to His disciples,

> But I tell you the truth, it is to your advantage that I go away; for if I do not go away, the Helper will not come to you; but if I go, I will send Him to you. And He, when He comes, will convict the world concerning sin and righteousness and judgment; concerning sin because they do not believe in Me; And concerning righteousness, because I go to the Father

and you no longer see Me; and concerning judgment, because the ruler of this world has been judged. I have many more things to say to you, but you cannot bear them now. But when He, the Spirit of truth, comes, He will guide you into all the truth; for He will not speak on His own initiative, but whatever He hears, He will speak; and He will disclose to you what is to come. He will glorify Me, for He will take of Mine and will disclose it to you. All things that the Father has been Mine; therefore, I said that He takes of Mine and will disclose it to you.

This scripture informs us about the Holy Spirit, whom the believer in Christ will have after the Messiah's passing on the cross.

Listening to what the pastor teaches in the sermon and reading the Bible by myself gives me a further understanding of the Trinity. It is fascinating to read the scriptures combined with the pastor's teaching in the church, and the Holy Spirit, who is in me, further guides me in understanding the gospel. Once again I was amazed by the Lord Jesus, who guides and teaches me through His Holy Spirit residing in me. I told myself, "Wow, Jesus is the one true God who says who He is and reveals Himself through God's Word, the Bible, with the Holy Spirit He promised to give once He left this earth."

7

THE DEEP CALLS UNTO DEEP

My HUNGER CONTINUED FOR MORE OF JESUS. IN March 2012, I fasted and prayed for twenty-one days. I enjoyed my personal worship and prayer time with God. During that time, I frequently invited one of my close Christian friends to fellowship with me. In my daily prayer, I asked the Holy Spirit to fill me with His power. I was fascinated with the miracles that the Lord Jesus did while He was on earth. The disciples the Lord Jesus called were all filled with His power, and I was amazed by the miracles of healing, casting out demons, and raising the dead to life that the disciples carried out.

To be honest, I was hungry to see the miracles that took place in the Bible happen today. When my fast ended, I was eager to continue with the fast for a total of forty days. I knew the Lord Jesus did a forty-day fast, and I had the desire to do what the Lord did. I started the fast in March and continued it beyond the Easter celebration. I had a strong desire to go on for forty days. At the time of the Easter celebration, I was still fasting, but I felt emotionally low. The first reason was that I could not attend church that morning due to my work. One of the hospitals I worked in had a policy that every nurse should work alternate weekends, and that was my weekend to work. I was feeling miserable, and besides that, I was also fasting.

When I prayed that morning, I told the Lord I felt unhappy because I had to work, and I was fasting on a day when I should have been getting together with my fellow Christians for dinner.

I usually abstain from going out to eat on my fasting days. I prepare my own food at home. I sacrifice breakfast and lunch, but I do drink water and have dinner. I told the Lord that if my fast had been for twenty-one days, I would not go beyond Easter Sunday, but I felt a strong desire to do a forty-day fast. I ended up feeling miserable this Easter because I was working and not able to feast with friends. Shortly after the prayer, I left for work.

At work, I did the usual stuff. I was assigned to a post–cardiac surgery patient. I was doing the normal things I do when helping the patient recover from cardiac surgery. The patient had a breathing tube in his mouth, he had recovered from anesthesia, and the surgery had been successful. I worked to remove the breathing tube from the patient. While the breathing tube was still in, the patient was wide awake, and he was trying to communicate with me. He was pointing to me with his right index finger.

I told him, "You can't talk now because you have a

breathing tube. We are working toward removing the tube, and once it is out, you can talk to me." He was an older adult, and he looked pleasant. Once again he wanted to talk, but I had to calm him down and call the respiratory therapist to help me get everything ready for the smooth removal of the breathing tube.

Once the respiratory therapist came in, we removed the breathing tube, and the patient appeared very cheerful. He seemed to be relieved after the removal of the breathing tube. The respiratory therapist left the room after the procedure was completed.

I started talking to the patient and gave him some instructions to ensure he knew the care plan. The patient started talking to me, and he looked overly excited despite being in pain postsurgery.

He said, "I can see you clearly."

I said, "Sure, you can see me; you don't have eye issues."

Then he said, "My right eye was 90 percent blind. When I opened my eyes this morning, I could see you clearly from both of my eyes. I was pointing my right index finger toward you while the breathing tube was in to inform you that I see you clearly."

I was skeptical and told him, "I don't see any diagnosis in the healthcare chart regarding your right eye problem."

He said there was very minimal vision in his right eye. He could not drive for many years, and he was denied a driver's license by the Department of Motor Vehicles. He continued to say that he had been very frustrated that he was not given the driver's license and wanted very badly to drive again. His primary physician had told him that he has macular degeneration in the right eye, and there was no cure for that.

When I went through his healthcare record for the second time, I found a macular degeneration history. The gentleman went on to close his left eye with his left hand, and he said he could clearly see the time on the clock on the wall with his right eye.

At that moment, I had goosebumps and stood rigidly for a few seconds. I told myself in my heart that today was Easter Sunday, the Lord Jesus was here, and He had shown His miraculous healing power.

I asked the gentleman whether he knew what day that Sunday was. He said it was Easter Sunday. I asked him, "Are you a Christian?"

He answered, "Yes, I am, and I attend Calvary Chapel Church near my home."

The patient asked for his family to come in right away. I said sure, and I knew they were out in the waiting room. His wife and son came in. The patient shared what had happened with his family.

His wife and son said it was true that he could not see in his right eye, but now he was able to see clearly. They cried once they knew that his eyesight had come back. The entire family was emotional with happy tears. The patient said he believed in Jesus, and he knew that Jesus was the healer on that day.

I shared my belief in Jesus and mentioned the church I attended.

The patient said, "The Lord must have honored you for working on this Easter Sunday. At the first touch of your hand on me, I opened my eyes while the breathing tube was in my mouth. I saw you very clearly, and instantly I was excited."

After he said that once again, I had goosebumps and teared up.

I remembered the prayer I had prayed that morning. I had had a conversation with the Lord about why I was still fasting and why I was working on Easter Sunday. I realized the Lord has His own way to show Himself, and He has His own way to make the patient's beloved face shine with inner happiness and peace.

The patient and his family invited me to visit them in their church once he was discharged. We exchanged our church addresses so that we could keep in touch in the future. That day was a historic day for me because I experienced more of the Lord Jesus, and I learned how the Holy Spirit moves in His people.

I said to myself, "Wow, what a healer the Lord Jesus is." I was amazed to experience what the Lord did in the Bible when He healed the blind. I saw myself as a vessel of conduit to transmit His healing touch. In Matthew 14:14, the scripture says, "And when Jesus went out He saw a great multitude, and He was moved with compassion for them and healed their sick."

In this patient's condition, he was desperate to drive his car. He had been denied his driver's license for many years, and the Lord Jesus knew that. He had compassion on that patient and healed him from macular degeneration, which has no cure today.

8

THE FAITH WALK

URING THE LAST QUARTER OF 2013, I ASKED THE LORD about my direction in life. *Is there anything more than this?* I seemed to have reached a plateau moment around the middle of 2013. I found nothing exciting at work or in my personal life except wanting to know more about Jesus and everything He had for me. I was still single, but that was not a problem. I knew my Savior has a plan for me, and whatever He has for me in this lifetime, that is what I will do.. I continued seeking God in my daily prayer and worship time with Him. After prayer, I asked God what He wanted to do in this life of mine. I wanted Him to give me further guidance and direction.

One day after work, I went to a Thai restaurant to buy dinner. While I was walking there, suddenly I heard the word *Detroit* in my head. I knew Detroit was a city in

America, but honestly I did not know where it was located on the map. After having dinner, I went home and looked at the map via Google search. I learned it is a city in Michigan located near the Great Lakes, in the Upper Midwest region of the United States.

I sought God further for the reason Detroit had come to my mind. As the day passed, I felt like I had to go to Detroit for my next destination in life with God.

I prayed and asked God for clarity of mind and whether Detroit was the next place I should live. As the day passed, I had the strong urge I should investigate the city of Detroit. After reading about Detroit on the Internet, I did not find anything interesting or extraordinary about that city, but I desired to go there.

By December 2013, my feeling was even stronger than before, so I started looking for a Detroit job. At the time, there were two hospitals that had vacancies in the critical care setting. I applied and told myself, *If I get a response, it will be a sign that I should leave California and go to Detroit.*

One of the hospitals wanted to conduct a telephone interview. I responded right away and gave the dates I would be available for the telephone interview. The telephone interview went well. After a short while, the human resource recruiter called me and said that I should come to Detroit to sign some papers. The manager of the unit and the recruiter would like to see me face-to-face. I said yes to that and gave them a date I could come.

Because it was the holiday season in December and many of the staff took turns to go on vacation, I finally visited Detroit in the third week of January 2014. While I was there, I came across another hospital. I was attracted to that hospital, and it looked like I might learn more and get more hands-on experience if I worked there.

The hospital that invited me to sign the papers did not force me to sign anything unless I was happy with the salary and the benefits they offered. I told them I would think about it and give them an answer if I agreed with what had been offered. They were kind enough to give me time, and no pressure was put on me.

Meanwhile, I applied to the other hospital I was attracted to. After a few days, I was called by the recruiter, who told me that the manager would like to have an interview via the phone. I gave the recruiter the dates I would be available, and an interview was scheduled. Soon after the interview, the manager called me, and I was offered a position. I declined the offer from the first hospital. I had peace in my heart, and I knew God was with me and was directing my path.

It took some time to complete all the paperwork and get the Michigan state license in nursing. By the time everything was complete, it was April 2014. At the end of April, I put in my resignation at the hospital in California. My manager did not expect that from me, and she wanted me to take a six-month break and come back fresh. I did not share why I had decided on the new job; I kept it between God and my close Christian friends.

I told my manager I had to leave, and I could not accept the offer to be away for six months and come back after that. I told her everything was okay, but I wanted to grow and experience more, and this was the best decision I could make for myself. She teared up, we hugged each other, and I left the organization after six years of service.

I was excited but at the same time fearful because it was going to be a new place for me, and I did not know what to expect. I talked to the Lord daily in my prayers, asking Him to protect and further guide me on this new journey. I also shared it with my pastor, and he was surprised and asked me, "Why Detroit?"

I told him how I had decided on Detroit, and he wanted me to keep in touch. The pastor's wife said she would visit me in Detroit once I had settled there. She prayed for me, and I moved on.

I started my life in Detroit in the second week of May 2014. Everything was going smoothly. Because I did not know anyone there, I googled to find a church to attend. I found a full gospel and Pentecostal church and started going there. The first time I attended the church, I felt the tremendous presence of the Lord, and instantly I knew this was the church for me. I did not have friends in Detroit, so I spent time fasting and seeking the Lord on all my days off. I was growing in my faith and enjoyed the intimate time with the Lord.

During the first month, it all went smoothly. In the second month, I felt a struggle with the workflow, the system, and the new people at my workplace. After my orientation, I was not happy at the workplace. The workflow seemed to be different from that in California. I gave myself time to get used to it. In California, I was working the day shift. I was on the night shift in Detroit, but that was not a big issue. I felt the workplace was so strange that I could not fit in as I had in California. It made me seek the Lord even more, and I asked for His wisdom to help me flow smoothly in my new workplace.

In November, I was very disturbed, and I even felt like I was a failure at my workplace. I was extremely uncomfortable with the setting, and the workflow was still a struggle. The weather was changing and becoming very cool, and I experienced snow for the first time on Thanksgiving Day. I liked snow, but I had difficulty adjusting to weather changes and driving in the snow. Loneliness was not an issue because the Lord was with me. The weather and the workplace were challenging for me, and I struggled to adjust to the changes.

In December, it was even worse. The weather was so much cooler, and it was snowing. I did not feel like working each time I drove to work, and I was emotionally disturbed. I did not feel like leaving my apartment. I made a few friends in Detroit, but I still felt a little depressed. I questioned myself as to whether I had made the right move. At that time, It was my seventh month in Detroit since moving from California. I was thinking a lot and crying a lot as well. Even though I was attending church regularly, I did not feel like doing anything else.

I was becoming increasingly isolated as the days went by. My prayer and worship time had surely increased. Prayer, worship, and reading the Word of God were the only activities that kept me alive inside. I was unhappy with everything except my love for Jesus, which had never changed. I continued praying and seeking the Lord, and I confessed to the Lord that I was unhappy and depressed in Detroit. I told my Lord I missed all my friends, my former coworkers, and the workplace in California.

After talking and wrestling with God in my prayer closet, I decided to leave Michigan and go back to California.

After I made that decision, I went to Florida and stayed with my friend whom God had used to bring me to Jesus for the first time in California. That friend had gone to live in Florida after a few years in California.

I decided to take a break and I stayed with her in Florida. I shared everything I was facing in Detroit. My heart was certainly unhappy, and I was becoming depressed. I told her I had failed in a God-given mission in my life with the results of my move to Detroit. I expressed my feeling of being a failure in my journey in the walk of faith.

My friend was kind, and she suggested that I move to Florida, and we would live as a family. I told her that I must move on in my life, but I did not want to move to Florida. The reason was that I did not want to move to another state without seeking God first. I told my friend I would go back to California.

I was also thinking that my parents were getting older, and they still needed to be saved. They were still Hindus in Malaysia. My dad was also experiencing knee pain due to aging, and I wanted to see him and help him get proper medical treatment in Malaysia.

I started looking into travel nursing opportunities. As a travel nurse, I would not be committed as full-time staff to a hospital but would have short contracts. I registered with a travel agency from Florida. I told the agency my preferences for where I would like to work. I was keen to go back to Southern California. The contract that I got was for thirteen weeks in Southern California, and I planned to go to Malaysia at the end of the contract. I planned to stay in Malaysia for two weeks and then start with a thirteen-week contract in any hospital in Southern California.

While I was in Florida with my friend, I planned my next steps. I signed a contract with the agency for thirteen weeks at one of the hospitals in Los Angeles, California. I felt relieved that I had my new job, and I was also excited because I would be able to go to Malaysia and spend time with my parents after the short contract ended.

I had a good break with my friend in Florida and felt refreshed. I also did a reflection every night about the move I had made in 2014 from California to Michigan and whether or not it was from God. I felt it was a mystery why I had made that change and failed to find rest in Michigan. I moved on despite the failure. I wanted to progress instead of being stagnant.

On January 2, 2015, after working in Michigan for about six months, I started the travel nursing job in Los Angeles, California. I performed the normal duties I used to do as a bedside nurse. In the second week of January 2015, I began a twenty-one-day fast. I was also looking for a church to attend. During the fast, I surrendered myself into the hands of Jesus once again. I wanted His guidance and His leading.

This time I was broken due to my recent failure in Michigan. I also had the feeling that I had not given enough time to getting used to the surroundings and the people there. What was most devastating was that I had failed to obey God. I said to myself, *If I had met more people there and become committed to a Bible study group, I would have made it.* It took me some time to let go of that bitter memory, but above all I had failed God.

I walked in shame and guilt in my heart and mind for many months. I met new people and made new friends in Los Angeles. I really liked the hospital I worked for. when my contract ended, and I signed another contract to work in the same hospital. My heart was at peace, and I continued to meet new people.

One drawback with the travel nursing in the hospital I was working for was the frequent floating or moving to other units. When the second contract had almost ended, one of the unit staff I worked with said, "Why don't you apply for a full-time job here? There is one opening for the night position."

I said I would like to, but I needed to go back to Malaysia after the second contract was completed to spend time with my parents. I said I would stay as a travel nurse.

Other staff members also encouraged me to apply for the full-time position. I prayed about it, and at the same time, I told my parents I would be coming home soon to visit and spend quality time with them.

Somewhere around July 2015, I dreamed that I was carrying a bag full of white rice, and it was spilling from the bag onto the floor. I also saw chocolates everywhere in the hospital I worked for. That dream signifies a positive sign which means abundance of provision, joy and happiness from the Lord. I have not sought for the interpretation of the dream but at that moment in my life, I knew the Lord was communicating to me via dream. Shortly after the dream, I decided to apply for a full-time position.

In a few days, I got a call for an interview. The unit manager said she knew me already, so the interview was more of a formality to follow recruitment procedures. She accepted me right away, but I told her I must go to Malaysia because I had aging parents I wanted to spend time with. I was granted a three-month leave of absence before I started the full-time position.

I was touched by what I had been granted and thanked God and gave Him glory for everything happening at that moment. I felt like it was the right time, the right people, and the right place. Shortly after I ended the travel contract, I signed up for a full-time position at that hospital and went to Malaysia. My heart was filled with joy and peace.

I did as many things as I could for my parents, and after one month, I came back to California and started working as a full-time nurse. At this point, my parents were still Hindu, they were not convinced that Jesus is the way to the Heavenly Father. I never gave up but persist in my daily prayer for their eyes to be open and their heart to be softened to come to the truth. Meanwhile, I was offered a much higher salary with the full-time position, and after one year, I went back to school and pursued a master of science in nursing.

When I reflected on my journey in this walk of faith, I heard that small still voice say, "The journey of moving to different places and roles was a test of faith." According to James 1:2, "Count it all joy when you fall in various trials, knowing that the testing of your faith produces patience." I see myself in that verse and also in Romans 8:28 that says, "All things work together for good to those who love God, to those who are the called according to His purpose." Peace and gladness filled my heart, and all the shame and guilt I had felt was gone.

9

~❧~

JOURNEY WITH MY LORD

$\mathcal{I}$ CONTINUED MY JOURNEY WITH MY LORD AND I surrendered everything into the hands of God. At this point in my life, obidience is everything. . As my relationship with the Lord grew closer and stronger, I wanted to present my body as a living sacrifice, holy, acceptable to God, which is my reasonable service (Romans 12:1). I did not want to conform to this world but sought to be transformed by the renewing of my mind, that I might prove what was the good and acceptable and perfect will of God (Romans 12:2).

Every morning I first seek the kingdom of God, and all the things I need in life shall be added (Matthew 6:33). I thank God when I open my eyes from a long night's sleep. I thank God for the very breath He is giving me and the good night's sleep He gave me last night. I remind myself always to rejoice, pray without ceasing, and to give thanks in everything, for this is the will of God in Christ Jesus for me (1 Thessalonians 5:16–18).

In every challenging situation I face in daily life, I tell myself not to be fearful because the Lord has not given me the spirit of fear but the spirit of power and love and a sound mind (2 Timothy 1:7). When I am anxious about something, I get into the mode of prayer in silence. The Lord taught me not to be anxious about anything, but in everything by prayer and supplication, with thanksgiving, I let my request be made known to God, and the peace of God that surpasses all understanding will guard my heart and mind through Christ Jesus (Philippians 4:6–7).

Despite situations that are chaotic and full of uncertainty, I know I must remain strong and of good courage, and I refuse to be afraid or be dismayed, for I know the Lord God is with me wherever I go (Joshua 1:9).

In a situation where I feel helpless, I go to my Lord Jesus right away to ask for help because I know without the shadow of a doubt that my help comes from the Lord, who made heaven and earth (Psalm 120:1). When I feel unwell and weak in my body, the Lord's grace is sufficient for me, for His strength is made perfect in my weaknesses (2 Corinthians 12:9).

Whenever my mind is troubled, I find comfort from the scripture that says my Lord has searched me and known me; He knows my sitting down and my rising; He understands my thought afar off (Psalm 139:1–2). What a powerful scripture that says the Lord knows it all. I will never know it all, and I cannot run away from the Spirit of God. Wherever I go, the Spirit of the Lord is there; if I ascend into heaven, He is there; if I make my bed in hell, behold He is there (Psalm 139:7–8). He is the God who created heaven and earth, and therefore nothing is impossible in God's hands (Luke 1:37). I can relate when one says the Lord is omnipotent, omnipresent, and omniscient because God's Word in the Bible confirms His attributes.

As I draw closer and closer to God, I have the confidence to answer anyone who has a question about all the events taking place in the universe. I tell them I do not have the answer for everything, but one thing for sure is that whatever the Lord pleases, He does in heaven and on earth, in the sea, and in all deep places (Psalm 135:6). As a Christian, I answer from a Christian perspective from God's Word.

Despite disasters that are happening right now and will happen in the future, I have no shame in sharing the gospel and the signs of the end-time mentioned in the Bible. Lord Jesus told His disciples about the signs of the end of the age, which include nations rising against nations and kingdoms rising against kingdoms. There will be famines, pestilences, and earthquakes in various places (Matthew 24:7). Meanwhile, the Lord gave me a mission before the end-time comes to write this book, whose goal is for all to come to know the Lord Jesus. The Lord said that the gospel of the kingdom would be preached in all the world as a witness to all the nations, and then the end will come (Matthew 24:14).

I may not have been called to preach the gospel, but God has His own ways to use a surrendered vessel to spread the good news. Therefore, I want to inform everyone reading this testimony to repent for the kingdom of heaven is at hand (Matthew 4:17). *Repent* in this passage means to change your mind or turn from sin. It also means looking at the past and changing your mind about the past. This scripture brought me back to the dreams I had when I first received Jesus into my heart. I had dreams about my past living as a Hindu, and the dream was repeated at least once. It took me some time to understand the dream. Then the revelation came to me that the Lord was leading me into a new life, and He was putting off the "old man" in me. In this dream, the Lord was affirming that He is the one true God, and nobody goes to the Father except through Jesus because He is the way, the truth, and the life (Matthew 14:6).

Many would say this is simply another story of conversion from Hinduism to Christianity. As far I am concerned, I was once upon a time hungry and searching for God, and wanted God to talk to me. It was Jesus who heard my cry and my desperation. He picked me up and gave me a new life, and we started a relationship. Jesus said in Matthew 7:7–8, "Ask, and it will be given to you; seek, and you will find; knock, and it will be opened to you; for everyone who asks receives, and he who seeks finds, and to him who knocks it will be opened." When I was searching for God and the deeper things in life, I did not realize I was seeking, asking, and knocking on the door, asking God to show up and communicate with me.

10

FOLLOWING THE LORD'S
PLANS AND PURPOSES

"*I* KNOW THE THOUGHTS THAT I THINK TOWARDS YOU, SAYS the Lord, thoughts of peace and not of evil, to give you a future and a hope" (Jeremiah 29:11). This verse convinced me that the Lord has everything planned for me. I seek the Lord in my daily prayer for what He wants me to do from day to day to ensure I am on track in fulfilling the heavenly Father's perfect will. I realized that all my plans must be surrendered into the hands of God as in James 4:13–15, "Come now, you who say, 'Today or tomorrow we will go to such and such a city, spend a year there, buy and sell, and make a profit'; whereas you do not know what will happen tomorrow. For what is your life? It is even a vapor that appears for a little time and then vanishes away.

Instead, you ought to say, 'If the Lord wills, we shall live and do this or that.'"

Even though I plan things, I am sensitive to the leading of the Holy Spirit. Being sensitive to the Holy Spirit comes by prayer, worship, reading, listening to the Word of God, and sometimes a short fast. In the ups and downs of life, I have learned to lean on the Lord and live in the fruit of the Spirit: love, joy, peace, goodness, kindness, faithfulness, gentleness, self-control, and not forgetting long-suffering (Galatians 6:22–23).

Following in the footsteps of the Lord Jesus, I have the confidence to say that my heart's desires will be fulfilled if I continue to delight in the Lord (Psalm 37:4). Furthermore, Jesus said in John 14:13–14, "And whatever you ask in My name, that I will do, that the Father may be glorified in the Son. If you ask anything in My name, I will do it." Wow, what comforting words by the Lord Jesus. For all the plans I have, I do not have the pressure of whether they will come to pass because ultimately the Lord will lead and guide me along this journey of my life and He makes it beautiful in His time (Ecclesiaites 3: 11) I have heard preachers say the Lord leads like the GPS we have when we drive on the road. God's plans and purposes are the best, and this is what I call a blessed life.

11

REFLECTING ON MY
LIFE'S JOURNEY

IN MY DAILY WALK WITH GOD, I MEDITATE UPON THE WORD of God. I know in my spirit that everything that happens in my life is not an accident. God knew me before He formed me in my mother's womb (Jeremiah 1:5), and therefore nothing happens without reason. It is not an accident to be born in a Hindu family. God ordains that, so I might be the firstborn in my family to lead them to the one true God, who is Jesus. Jesus said in John 8:12, "I am the light of the world. He who follows Me shall not walk in darkness, but have the light of life." Therefore, the Lord has made me be the light as well because Matthew 5:16 says, "Let your light so shine before men, that they may see your good works and glorify your Father in heaven."

Becoming a nurse twenty-five years ago was God's plan

as well. God let me see the suffering of human beings with diseases, and I asked the Lord to anoint me with the gift of healing so I could pray for the sick. By working as a nurse in an organization, I take it seriously as a mission that God gave me to transmit love and care to everyone I come across, especially the patients that I care for that day. When a patient asks me what makes me joyful and very caring in everything I do, my answer is always that Jesus gave me this job, He fills me daily, and I cannot hold back but must give it away. The fear of God ensures I do everything thoroughly because whatever I sow, I reap (Galatians 6:7).

I also remember very well how, in my early life, I asked why some people are born blind, deaf, without arm and legs, and with many congenital health problems. I found the answer in John 9:2–3, where the disciples asked Jesus, "Rabbi, who sinned, this man or his parents, that he was born blind?" Jesus answered, "Neither this man nor his parents sinned, but that the works of God should be revealed in him."

Jesus also called His disciples, including all believers, to go into all the world and preach the gospel to every creature (Mark 16:15). Besides that, the Lord equips His servants with spiritual gifts to accomplish His task on earth, and one of the gifts is the gift of healing. The spiritual gifts are mentioned in 1 Corinthians 12.

I see my future as finishing strong in my faith because the Lord is the author and finisher of my faith (Hebrew 12:2). The apostle Paul said in Philippians 1:21, "For me, to live is Christ, and to die is gain." I have learned to practice that principle in my life as well. The best thing is that I know where I will be after this life ends because the Lord said in John 14:1–2, "Let not your heart be troubled; you believe in God, also believe in Me. In my Father's house are many mansions; if it were not so, I would have told you. I go to prepare a place for you."

I have chosen to walk the narrow path in my life. According to Matthew 7:13, "Enter by the narrow gate: for wide is the gate and broad is the way that leads to destruction, and there are many that go in by it." Whatever I do in my life, I do it for the glory of God (1 Corinthians 10:31).

I have used the word *wow* numerous times in this testimony, and I am still amazed at the Lord as if I was born again just yesterday. Life is short, and I hope to live life to the fullest following Jesus and all that He has for me. It is truly fulfilling, and it is difficult for me to find the right words to describe the joy of walking this life on earth. I am looking forward to eternity as well because now I know who I am, whom I belong to, and why I am here.

Once again, I want to say, "Wow, what a transformation of life." If searching for the deeper things in life is also your desire, and you do not know which direction you are heading in, I urge you to say this prayer aloud: "I ask Jesus to come into my heart and be Lord over my life." Then you can experience the one true living God and the abundance of life in Jesus.

Romans 10:9 says, "If you confess with your mouth the Lord Jesus and believe in your heart that God has raised Him from the dead, you will be saved." Meanwhile, in Romans 3:23 it is written, "For all have sinned and fall short of the glory of God." The Lord Jesus is the Good Shepherd;

He came so that we may have life and that we may have it more abundantly (John 10:10). May the Lord bless you and keep you. Amen.

Printed in the United States
by Baker & Taylor Publisher Services